Boots and Shoes

written by
Ann Cooper

KAEDEN ❤ BOOKS™

Table of Contents

Fishing Boots 5
Climbing Boots 6
Sandals 7
Rain Boots 8
Cowboy Boots 10
Ballet Shoes. 11
Ski Boots 12
Athletic Shoes 13
Glossary 15
Index 16

There are many kinds of boots and shoes.

Fishing Boots

fishing pole

net

Some boots are made for **fishing** in the river.

5

Climbing Boots

spikes

Some boots are made for climbing mountains.

Sandals

Some shoes are made for walking over the sand.

7

Rain Boots

Some boots are made for splashing through puddles.

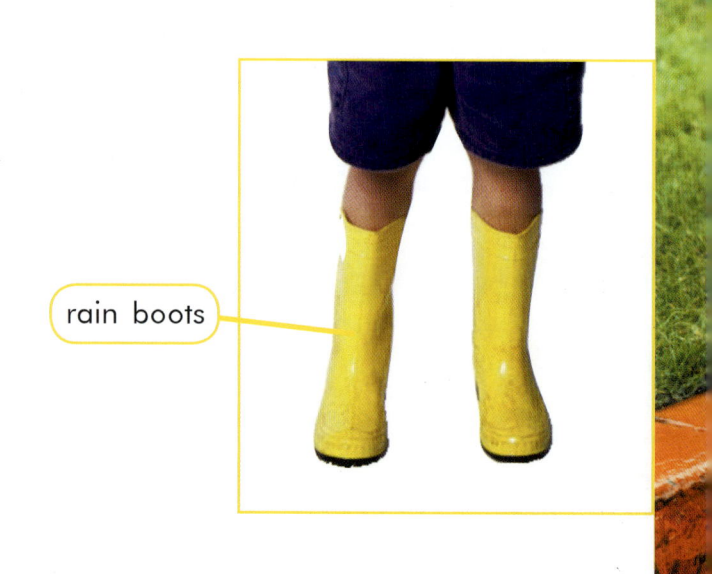

rain boots

9

Cowboy Boots

cowboy boots

Some boots are made for riding a horse.

Ballet Shoes

Ballet shoes are also called ballet slippers.

Some shoes are made for dancing on the **stage**.

11

Ski Boots

helmet

pole

ski

Some boots are made for **skiing** in the snow.

Athletic Shoes

There are many names for athletic shoes including tennis shoes, sneakers, trainers and gym shoes.

Some shoes are made for running in the park.

13

Which pair is right for me?

14

Glossary

fishing – the act or technique of catching fish

skiing – the sport of gliding on skis

stage – a raised platform on which people perform or speak

Index

boots 4, 5, 6, 8, 10, 12

climbing 6

dancing 11

fishing 5

horse 10

me 14

mountains 6

pair 14

park 13

puddles 8

riding 10

river 5

running 13

sand 7

shoes 4, 7, 11, 13

skiing 12

snow 12

splashing 8

stage 11

walking 7